THE NATURE EXPLORER'S DRAWING GUIDE FOR KIDS

Step-by-Step Lessons for Observing and Drawing Animals, Plants, and Insects

KRYSTAL AND BRAD WOODARD

of the

BRAVE KIDS
✕ ART CLUB ✕

The Nature Explorer's Drawing Guide for Kids:
Step-by-Step Lessons for Observing and Drawing Animals, Plants, and Insects

Brad and Krystal Woodard
Brave Kids Art Club

Editor: Kelly Reed
Project manager: Lisa Brazieal
Marketing coordinator: Katie Walker
Copyeditor: Patricia Pane
Interior layout: Aren Straiger
Cover production: Aren Straiger
Cover artwork: Brad Woodard

ISBN: 978-1-68198-993-8
1st Edition (1st printing, July 2023)
© 2023 Brave the Woods
All images © Brad Woodard unless otherwise noted.

Rocky Nook Inc.
1010 B Street, Suite 350
San Rafael, CA 94901
USA

www.rockynook.com

Distributed in the UK and Europe by Publishers Group UK
Distributed in the U.S. and all other territories by Publishers Group West

Library of Congress Control Number: 2022946087

CONTENTS

About the
AUTHOR AND ILLUSTRATOR

Brad Woodard is a professional illustrator, teacher, and the host of Brave Kids Art Club online show and classes. Growing up, Brad spent whatever time he wasn't drawing, outdoors exploring. His curiosity fueled his creativity, which only furthered his love for learning.

Brad and his wife, Krystal, the author of this book, started Brave Kids Art Club in hopes of offering a resource for kids to learn to be more confident, curious, and talented artists...and humans. Brave Kids Art Club is an online drawing learning resource for kids, where Brad teaches kids that everybody can learn to draw and have a lot of fun doing it! Brad not only teaches basic drawing techniques, but also how to explore and learn about the fascinating world around us!

Brad and Krystal also run a creative agency called Brave the Woods, whose focus is making fun educational products for both kids and those who are kids at heart. He's designed for major brands, children's books, animations, toys, and more!

BRAVE KIDS
✕ ART CLUB ✕

Find out more about Brave Kids Art Club at:

www.bravekidsartclub.com

www.bravethewoods.com

5

Introduction to
EXPLORING NATURE

In order to draw the world around us, we need to experience the world around us!

Getting out into nature and exploring is the best way to observe nature. There are plants, animals, and insects everywhere in the world (even in the city) if you know where to look. Bring your adventure backpack and take field notes everywhere you go!

Explorer Rules

✖ **Always ask permission or take an adult with you.**

✖ **Don't touch animals you find, just observe them.**

✖ **Keep a safe distance from wild animals.**

✖ **Do not disturb or destroy an animal's habitat.**

✖ **If you catch an insect for observation, do not keep it for long. Release it where you found it.**

Adventure Pack List

Pencil

Sketchbook

Eraser

Dark marker or pen

Colors: Markers, crayons, or colored pencils

Bonus Gear:

Magnifying glass

Binoculars

Camera

Observation jar with holes

Scientists Drew Their World

Scientists have been drawing the things they see and discover since humans began exploring the Earth. Early scientists didn't have photos, and there was a chance the specimens they collected wouldn't make it home, so they drew the things they found. Drawing has been an important method of recording and exploration for scientists throughout history.

CHARLES DARWIN, THE NATURALIST

Scientists who study the natural world are called Naturalists. One of the most famous naturalists was Charles Darwin. Darwin drew very detailed sketches of the living things he found on his scientific explorations throughout the world. The things he learned help us today to understand the natural world better.

ASKING EXPLORATIVE QUESTIONS

The more you learn about what you are seeing, the better you will be able to draw it. To learn, you must ask questions. Asking explorative questions helps us understand why the thing we are observing is the way it is.

How do we ask explorative questions? First, we have to gather information. These are some examples of exploratory questions:

What am I observing?

Is it living? Is it an animal, plant, or insect?

What makes it unique?

Is that unique aspect important?

How can I identify it?

Where did I find it?

What is its habitat?

By asking these kinds of questions, you are well on your way to being a scientist like Darwin!

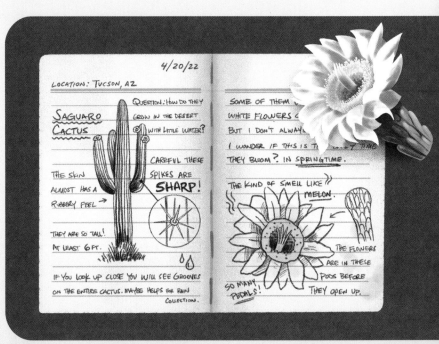

Drawing Techniques and Tips

BUILDING WITH SHAPES

Drawing things in nature can be difficult if you don't break down complex shapes into simple shapes first. You start by looking for basic shapes, build your form, and then add the details later. Going step by step makes the whole process much less intimidating.

Here are some example drawings of building an animal with shapes.

Detailed cardinal reference

Look for basic shapes in animals

Refine shapes while drawing

Simplify hard shapes

COLORING

Once you finish your drawing, it's time to color! You can mimic nature and make it accurate to your reference, or you can create something that has never been seen before. Have fun with it! Regardless of what you choose, here are a couple of techniques to get you started.

Color Layering

When coloring it is good to start with your lightest colors first, and then layer your darker colors on top. This can help you leave room for highlights and build up shadows to help your artwork look more dimensional.

Color Blending

The way you physically blend your colors depends on what type of coloring utensil you are using. If you are using tools like crayons or colored pencils, you blend colors by gradually applying more and more pressure as you overlap colors. The harder you press down the darker (more opaque) your color will be, and vice versa. If you use markers, you can simply use color layering.

Color Gradients

When you gradually transition, or blend, one color into another color, it is called a gradient. You can use two different colors, or use one color gradually applying less pressure to make it lighter and lighter. It's a great way to practice your blending and shading skills. Try it out!

Example of color gradients

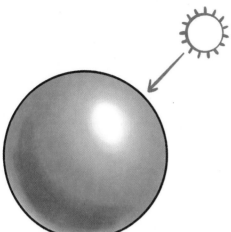

Highlights and Shadows

Adding these will help your drawings have depth and dimension. Highlights are areas where light is directly shining. Shadows are areas that are blocked from the light. With that in mind, decide where your light is coming from and stick with that the entire time you are coloring.

EXAMPLE:
Look at this snail. Can you tell where the light is coming from? Adding both highlights and shadows on the shell help it look less flat and more dimensional.

Analogous Colors

A good rule for blending is to use colors next to each other on the color wheel, or analogous colors. They will blend very easily with one another if you pick one direction on the color wheel and follow it. Like this flower for example, look at how the tips of the petals are yellow, and slowly we add oranges and eventually reds in the center.

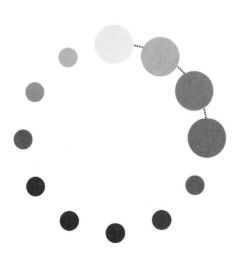

Color wheel example

ANIMAL PARTS

Some parts of animals can be tricky to draw, but understanding their anatomy can help! That way you can either draw every single detail, or keep it super simple, and still have it look like the animal you are drawing because you included their most identifying features.

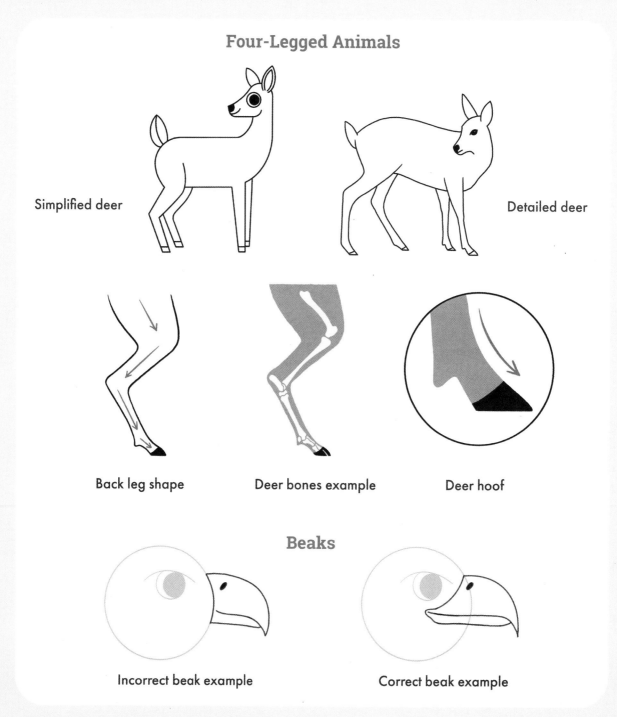

Four-Legged Animals

Simplified deer

Detailed deer

Back leg shape

Deer bones example

Deer hoof

Beaks

Incorrect beak example

Correct beak example

TEXTURES AND PATTERNS: FUR, FEATHERS, SCALES

Remember, you don't always have to draw every single detail (but you can if you want). Even just a few feathers, tufts of fur, or a handful of scales gets the idea across without having to actually draw them all.

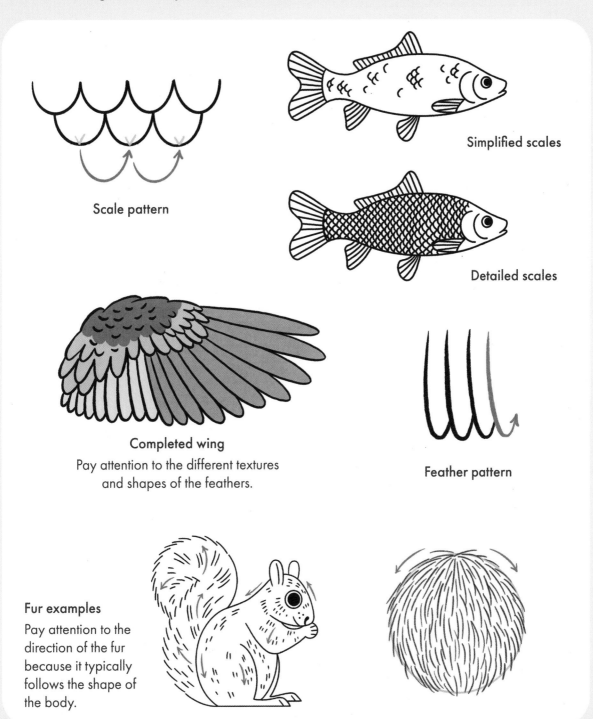

Scale pattern

Simplified scales

Detailed scales

Completed wing
Pay attention to the different textures and shapes of the feathers.

Feather pattern

Fur examples
Pay attention to the direction of the fur because it typically follows the shape of the body.

LET'S DRAW
GUIDE

Are you ready to draw? Great! Go grab your pencil and make sure you have an eraser handy—we are going to be doing a lot of erasing. Okay, let's get started!

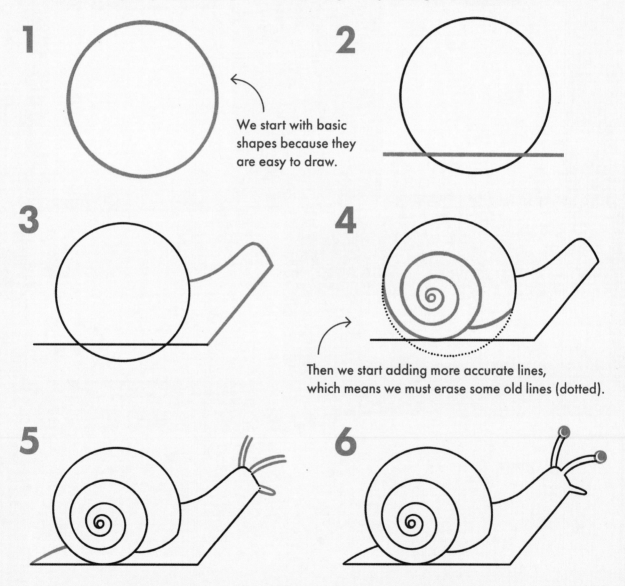

1 We start with basic shapes because they are easy to draw.

2

3

4 Then we start adding more accurate lines, which means we must erase some old lines (dotted).

5

6

TIP: Draw everything with a pencil first! Once you are happy with your sketch, you can outline it with a dark marker or pen to finalize it.

Final

Now color it in! If you want you can copy these colors or you can choose your own. Use crayons, markers, paint, or whatever. Have fun!

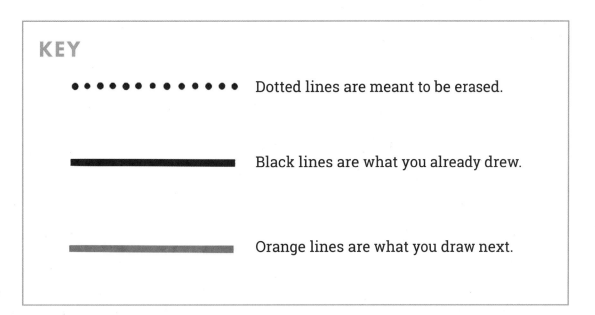

Let's draw a...
DEER

1

2

3
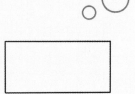

4
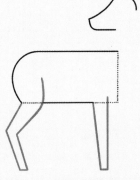

5
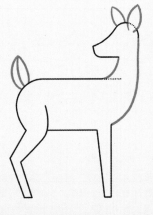

6

CRITTER PROFILE

A deer is a hoofed herbivore (meaning they eat plants) found almost everywhere in the world. Although there are many kinds of deer, they all share characteristics that will help you identify them. Deer have two hooves on each foot. This is called a cloven, or split, hoof. They all have long, thin legs, and a short tail. Their fur can be brown, reddish, or gray.

OBSERVATIONS

Male deer have antlers that are most noticeable when they are over a year old. They shed and re-grow these antlers each year. Deer antlers are one of the fastest-growing bones on any animal.

If you are lucky enough to spot a fawn (baby deer), you will notice white spots all over their backs that help to camouflage deer even better while they are young.

Deer are masters of disguise and easily blend in with the leaves and trees, so they can be hard to spot. A good rule of thumb is to sit very still and watch for any movement like a tail flick or head peeking around a tree.

TIP:

An evening walk with your family is a great time to look for deer! They sleep most of the day, but get up to eat in the evenings, so you may catch them grazing in a field or a yard, or right at the tree line.

Let's draw a...

BEAVER

1

2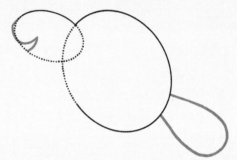

3

4

5

6

CRITTER PROFILE

Beavers are one of the largest animals in the rodent family. They are semiaquatic, meaning they live partially in water and on land. They are typically stocky (short and wide) to conserve heat and are covered in a thick layer of fat under their fur that keeps them warm in cold water. Their fur can be yellow-brown to black and they have large webbed back feet and small front paws with finger-like digits.

OBSERVATIONS

Beavers are most well known for their big flat tail covered in dark leathery scales that they use to swim, communicate, and even to prop themselves up.

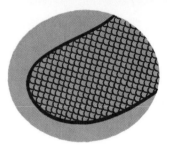

Beavers have long yellow front teeth that never stop growing, but daily use keeps them from getting too long. You can tell they are nearby if you see these signs: gnawed wood with teeth marks, felled trees (trees that have been cut down by a beaver chewing around the trunk), decorticated sticks (sticks with the bark removed), lodges, and dams.

Lodges are the dome-shaped homes beavers build out of sticks and mud. These are located on the edge of the water. Another structure beavers create are dams. This is a spot where they have built a wall to slow or stop running water and create a pond.

TIP:

Never go near or try to enter a beaver dam or lodge and never approach a beaver if you see them. They are territorial and don't like anyone near them or their homes. As always, make sure you have a grown-up with you when exploring, especially near water.

Let's draw a...
SQUIRREL

1

2

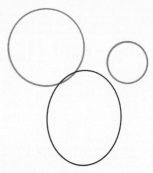

3

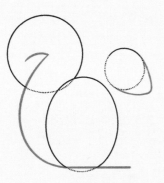

4

5

6

20

CRITTER PROFILE

There are over 260 species of squirrels that can be found almost everywhere (except Antarctica). This means that there are an estimated 4–10 billion squirrels on the Earth! Squirrels come in many shapes, sizes, and colors, but all can be identified by their strong hind legs, small hand-like forepaws, pointed ears, and large bushy tails.

OBSERVATIONS

Squirrels have four chisel-like front teeth, sharp claws, and usually four sets of whiskers (under the lower jaw, both above and below the eyes, and beside the nose) that they use to get information about the world around them.

Squirrels also have large black eyes with excellent peripheral vision that allow them to see things above, to the left, and to the right without moving their head. This makes it tricky to sneak up on a squirrel.

The best way to tell a squirrel from other rodents is its big bushy tail. Squirrel tails are very useful. They use it as a sunshade in summer, a blanket in the winter, an umbrella for snow and rain, a tool for balancing, and even for communication.

Squirrels can be arboreal, meaning they live in nests in trees, or terrestrial, meaning they live in burrows in the ground, so depending on the kind of squirrel you are looking for, you might want to keep an eye on both.

TIP:
If you are looking for squirrels in the spring and summer when the trees are full of leaves, don't look at the tree, stand under it and look up. You might see movement on the branches, or even catch a squirrel dropping seeds as it eats.

Let's draw a...
FOX

1

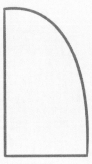

2

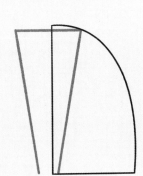

3

4

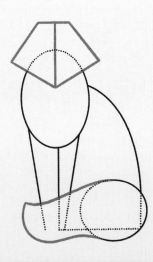

5

6

Foxes are versatile animals that can live in almost all kinds of habitats, from forests to deserts. They have long thick hair that varies depending on where they live and can either act as insulation in the cold or protect them from the hot ground. They have short legs with paws just like a dog and a narrow snout.

⊘BSERVATIONS

Foxes have large, pointed ears that allow them to have great hearing and radiate body heat to keep them cooler. They also have catlike eyes with vertical slit pupils so they can see well day or night.

Foxes are very good at blending in with their environment and can even change color to blend in better. The arctic fox is found in the far northern hemisphere and changes from brown in the summer to white like the snow in the winter.

Foxes live in burrows, also known as dens, that they dig out of the ground. These burrows provide a cool, safe place to sleep, store food, and keep their babies, called pups, protected. They like to dig their dens near where humans live, because then other predator animals like coyotes are more likely to leave them alone.

TIP:
Learning about the kind of fox that lives in your area, and its characteristics, will increase the chance of seeing one. The more you know what to look for, the better your chances.

Let's draw a...
RACCOON

1

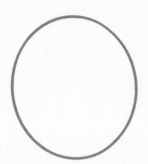

2

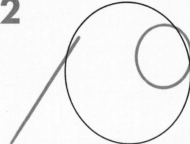

3

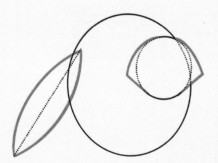

4

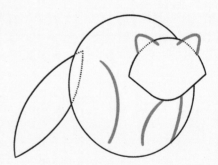

5

6

CRITTER PROFILE

Raccoons are mischievous omnivores (meaning they eat plants and animals) that live all over the United States. Raccoons have great eyesight, smell, and hearing. Their snout is long and thin with a black nose and white whiskers on the end. Raccoons have long furry banded tails with alternating stripes. These stripes may protect them by confusing predators to attack their tails instead of their bodies, making it easier for them to escape.

OBSERVATIONS

Raccoon masks might make them look like a bandit, but they are actually to help them see better by absorbing light, much like the black paint or strips that athletes sometimes wear under their eyes.

Raccoon hind legs are longer than their front legs, which makes them look hunched when on all fours, but allows them to stand on their hind legs only and use their front legs more like arms and hands. Raccoon paws are very hand-like, and sensitive. They use them like another set of eyes to identify items and can use them to open locks and even solve puzzles!

Raccoons like to live in wooded areas but can be found anywhere that they can create a den. In the woods, a den can be a hollowed-out tree, or a burrow abandoned by another animal. But, in more urban areas, raccoons are resourceful and will use anything as a den from a storm drain, chimney, mine, attic, or even abandoned cars.

TIP:

Raccoons are nocturnal, so the time to spot one is at night. While raccoons are not aggressive, and usually will not attack a person since they are scared of people, it is smart to observe them from a distance. Raccoons carry deadly diseases that can be easily spread to people.

Let's draw a...
RABBIT

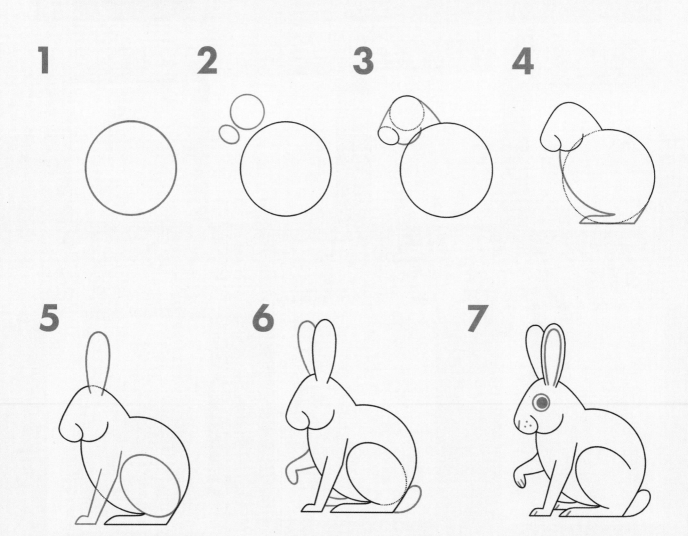

1

2

3

4

5

6

7

CRITTER PROFILE

Rabbits can be found all over the world in the wild and are also often kept as pets. They are small, egg-shaped animals covered in fur, with small front legs and large, strong hind legs made for hopping, and small fluffy tails. They have long ears that usually stand up (with exception of some breeds used only as pets). Rabbits can be a lot of different colors, including white, gray, brown, tan, black, and reddish with many spots and patterns.

OBSERVATIONS

Their ears allow them to hear extremely well – much better than a human. Rabbit ears can rotate 270 degrees, which is three-quarters of a circle, to listen to everything around them and detect if there are dangers nearby. Rabbits also use their ears to regulate their body temperatures.

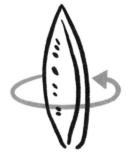

Rabbits have two sharp front teeth on top with two shorter teeth on bottom that are perfect for cutting and chewing on plants, twigs, and bark.

Rabbits can be found in all kinds of climates and biomes. They dig their homes, called warrens, in the ground and create an underground tunnel system with multiple entrances and exits, and rooms for sleeping. These tunnels allow them to escape quickly from predators. Cottontail rabbits, however, live in nests in hidden areas like hollowed-out logs and brush piles.

TIP:
Rabbits use their ears to communicate with body language, so watching a rabbit's ears is a good way to learn what they are feeling and what is going on around them. Ears up mean they are alert and listening, slightly back is relaxed, and pointed back means danger and that they are scared.

Let's draw a...

BEAR

1

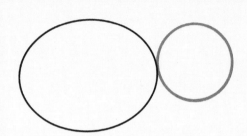

2

3

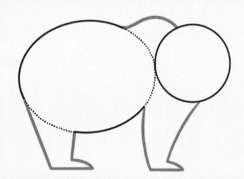

4

5

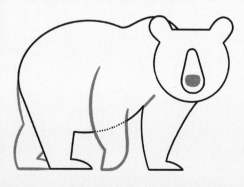

6

Bears are large furry animals with big furry bodies, short tails, and stocky legs. They have small, rounded ears and long snouts for great hearing and extra impressive smelling ability. Bears have large paws with five long claws on each paw. Their stocky legs help them run, climb, and swim very well. In North America, bears can range between 6 and 9 feet tall depending on the type and can weigh from 200 to 1,400 pounds!

⌕ OBSERVATIONS

Bear claws are specially adapted to digging for food, scratching bark, and catching prey. A bear's claws can be seen in its footprint and used to identify the kind of bear track it is.

Bears live in dens, which can be any sheltered area that can protect them while hibernating. Dens can be caves or rock crevices, hollow trees, and large fallen logs, dug-out tree roots, and even abandoned barns and buildings.

Bears hibernate, so they are not around when the temperature gets cold. During hibernation, their body temperature drops and they go into a deep sleep, living off the fat they gained in the fall before hibernating. Surprisingly, bears don't sleep this whole time, and wake periodically during hibernation to move around their den, eat, and go to the bathroom.

TIP:

If camping or hiking with your family in a place where bears live, your grown-up should always carry bear spray. Also, keep your food away from the campsite and locked up, or tied up high. If you find a bear den, or evidence that a bear is in the area such as fresh bear scat (poop), leave that area.

Let's draw a...

MOOSE

1

2

3

4

5

6

7

CRITTER PROFILE

Moose are the largest member of the deer family. They can grow to be almost 7 feet tall and weigh up to 1,500 pounds. They have dark, brownish-black fur and the males have large antlers. They have a shoulder hump from their large shoulder muscles and a flap of skin called a dewlap or bell below their chin. Moose have long, rounded snouts with wide nostrils that are perfect for locating smells.

OBSERVATIONS

Moose have palmate antlers (which means their antlers are shaped like an open hand instead of like twigs). Their antlers can be 4- to 5-feet wide, and they use them to protect themselves from predators and fight with other moose.

Moose have long legs and cloven hooves. This helps them run fast and swim well. Moose are made for cold weather with their thick coats and adapted hooves. Their hooves are wide like snow-shoes to help them walk in the snow.

Moose live in forested areas and can often be found near bodies of water. A good indicator that moose are in an area is rubbed trees with spots of bark missing from the rubbing of moose antlers.

TIP:
Moose are great animals to observe at a distance. They are not afraid of people and won't run away if spotted. However, don't approach a moose, because while they are not typically aggressive, they are huge animals that can be very dangerous if they feel threatened.

Let's draw a...

SKUNK

1

2

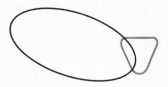

3

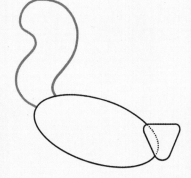

4

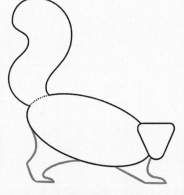

5

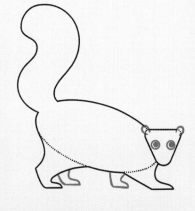

6

A skunk is a small, cat-sized animal that is found all over North and Central America. The most common kind of skunk is the striped skunk, which is black with two white stripes running from its head, all the way down its bushy tail that resembles a V, and a thin white stripe running from the forehead to its snout. Other types of skunks can have spots, swirls, or even solid-colored fur.

OBSERVATIONS

Their paws are partially webbed with long front claws. This trait makes them excellent diggers. Skunks dig to find food in the dirt, like grubs and other insects, and to make their burrows.

Skunks dig their burrows very deep so a predator can't see their nest from the outside. These burrows are usually found under rocks, logs, or even decks that can offer them more protection.

Skunks have small triangular heads and little round ears. They hunt by smell and sound and have very poor eyesight. Because of this, they are easily startled and have developed a stinky defense mechanism.

If you come across a skunk, it will first stomp its feet at you and arch its back. This means run because you don't want what comes next. If you still don't leave it alone, the skunk will spray a smelly fluid in your direction (up to 12 feet). This can sting the eyes of a predator and the stink can last a few weeks. They prefer not to spray but will if they feel threatened.

TIP:
If you smell skunk, and see small holes, watch out so you don't accidentally surprise one!

Let's draw a...
BAT

1

2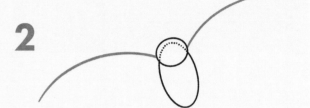

3

4

5

6

CRITTER PROFILE

Bats are the only flying mammals and are found most places in the world. There are more than 1,400 species of bats in the world, varying in size from a 6-inch wingspan to a 5-foot wingspan. Despite there being so many kinds, all bats share some basic features, such as fur-covered bodies, large ears, and webbed wings.

OBSERVATIONS

A bat's wings are made from webbed skin extending between its long, hollow "finger" bones, and connecting to its legs. They can move their wings just like we move our hands, which allows them to flap and twist their wings to lift and help them maneuver better in the air.

Bats are nocturnal and make their homes as a colony (large group) during the day in enclosed places like caves, bridges, building eaves or attics, crevices in rocks, and trees. Wooden bat houses are also great to watch at dusk for your chance to see a bat.

Bats have large ears that they use to see and navigate the world around them with echolocation (using sound waves from a noise they make to know where objects, such as food, are). A bat's ears are big and pointed, located on top of their heads, and have more than 20 muscles to help them move them around.

TIP:
The best time to see a bat is at dusk in the warmer months when they emerge together to hunt. Never catch or pick up a bat. They can and likely will bite and carry many dangerous diseases.

Let's draw a...

ROBIN

1

2

3

4

5

6

The American Robin is one of the most common birds in the US. Robins are grayish-black or brown with dark heads and an orange-red breast and white under their long tail feathers. They have white around their eyes and bright yellow beaks with a black tip. Female robins are less vibrant, with paler colors and lighter heads.

⚲BSERVATIONS

Robins have long legs and feet with four claws. When they land, they bend their legs and wrap their claws around a branch to clamp down and steady themselves.

Robins eat insects such as worms and beetles, and can be seen using their straight, thin beaks to dig in the dirt and pull bugs out. They also eat fruit and berries, and their beaks are great for stripping the skins off fruit. Their beak is not built to crack seeds, though, so you won't see them in a bird feeder.

Robins typically build their nests in the bottom half of a tree, shielded by leaves. These nests are built from grasses, twigs, and other found materials that a female robin weaves into a bowl shape with her beak and wings to form the shape. She then lays three to five small blue eggs in the nest in the spring.

TIP:
You can tell a Robin is nearby by listening for their song. Their song is described as 10 lilting whistles (rising and falling tones) and some even say it sounds like the robin is singing "cheer up."

Let's draw a...

BLUE JAY

1

2

3

4

5

6

The Blue Jay is a medium-sized bird found in the Eastern half of the United States and Canada. Like their name suggests, they are a striking blue color on their top and tail. Blue jays have white bellies and throats and a black necklace. Their wings and tail have black, white, and blue stripes, or bands. Blue jays have a blue crest, or crown, on the top of their head, that raises or flattens depending on their mood.

OBSERVATIONS

Blue jays have short, sharp, black beaks that are made specifically for cracking shells. Their beaks are made to be like a Swiss Army Knife. They use it to catch and pick up insects, crack seeds, pick up berries, and even as a tool for pushing seeds and nuts in the ground to store for later.

Blue jays have black legs and feet with four long toes on each foot. One toe faces backward to allow blue jays to securely wrap their feet around a branch to perch.

Blue jays are closely related to robins, and their nests and eggs look almost the same, except a blue jay egg is light blue with gray or brown spots.

Blue jays make a bunch of different calls, and sometimes even mimic birds like hawks, to scare other birds away from a bird feeder or other food source that they want.

TIP:
If you live in the Eastern half of the US, you can attract blue jays by hanging bird feeders with nuts and seeds.

Let's draw a...

CROW

1

2

3

4

5

6

CRITICAL PROFILE

Crows are large (17–21 inches) black birds that can be found in every state except Alaska and Hawaii. Crows are stocky and have a wingspan of about 3 feet. They are black from beak to tail with black legs and feet.

OBSERVATIONS

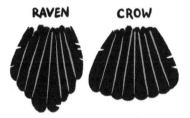

RAVEN   CROW

A crow's tail fans out when they fly, displaying their even-length tail feathers. This is how you tell them from ravens (which have a triangle tail). When a crow lands, they will often fan their tail out one to three times depending on their mood.

Crows have slim, straight, black beaks. They use their beaks to pick up and tear their food and crack nuts. They will eat just about anything, from berries and nuts, fruits and vegetables out of the garden, insects, fish, crabs, rodents, and reptiles, to even your leftover lunch.

When looking for crows, look high in the trees. They tend to build their nests toward the top of a tree. The best place to spot a crow is in gardens, farmland, and dumpsters. This is why farmers traditionally use "scarecrows" to try and scare the crows away from their crops.

TIP:
Crows make a raspy "caw" call. They can be found on their own, but most prefer to find food in groups, so listen for their calls, as they are noisy together.

Let's draw an...

EAGLE

1

2

3

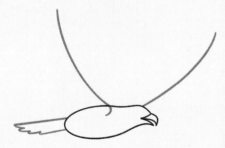

4

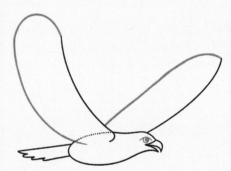

5

6

CRITTER PROFILE

The bald eagle is the national emblem of the United States and is significant to the Native American people. They can be found everywhere in North America and symbolize courage, freedom, and strength. Bald eagles are large birds (30 to 31 inches) and have a massive 6- to 7-foot wingspan. Despite their name, bald eagles are not actually bald and have white feathers on their entire head, shoulders, and tail.

OBSERVATIONS

Bald eagles have a hooked beak that is constantly growing. They use their beak for everything from building their giant (4- to 6-feet wide) nests, to preening (cleaning) their feathers, to tearing apart their food.

Bald eagles have pink tongues that look just like ours. Their tongues are special and have lots of receptors that sense things about what they are eating, such as pressure, texture, and temperature. They also have barbs on their tongues that pull food to the back of their mouths.

Bald eagles' super-strong talons are another tool they have for catching prey. Their feet are smaller than a hand, but 10 times stronger than an adult man's grip, and covered in thick yellow skin with sharp black talons at the end. They can snatch up their prey and carry up to 8 pounds back to their nest to eat. Bald eagles can fly 30 mph and can reach speeds of up to 100 mph when diving to catch their prey.

TIP:
The best state to see a Bald Eagle is Alaska, where their population is about 30,000.

Let's draw a...

MALLARD

1

2

3

4

5

6

CRITTER PROFILE

Mallards are medium-sized waterfowl that live everywhere in the world, except Antarctica. The male mallard, or drake, is very recognizable for their colorful feathers – especially their bright-green heads. Their head and neck is an iridescent green (meaning the colors change or shimmer at different angles) with a white wing at the base. Their bodies are covered in gray, brown, and white feathers with a black-and-white tail.

⌕OBSERVATIONS

Drakes have yellow bills with a black tip. Their bills are rounded at the tip and made of bones that are covered with a fleshy material. The edges of the bill are soft so they can use it like a fingertip to find their food by feel.

The black tip on their bill is like a fingernail that they use to move and hook food. The inner edges of the bill are covered in lamellae, a comb-like line that looks like small teeth. They use these as a strainer to get their food out of mud and dirty water. They eat seeds, roots, and stems of plants, and eat insects, frogs, small fish, and crustaceans living in the water.

When migrating, mallards can fly 4,000 feet up in the air, but have been known to fly as high as 21,000 feet in altitude (as high as airplanes) and are one of the highest-flying animals.

TIP:
Don't offer bread to ducks to get them to come to you. Bread overfills their bellies and can lead to them not getting enough nutrients, which can cause sickness and death.

Let's draw an...

OWL

1

2

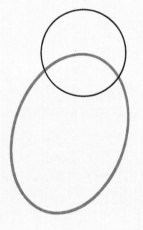

3

4

5

6

CRITTER PROFILE

Owls are nocturnal birds with large heads in comparison to their stocky bodies and short tail. They can be tiny like the elf owl, or big like the great horned owl. They are covered in soft, thick feathers of varying colors that are specially designed for silent stealthy flight. Owls have sharp, hooked beaks and flat faces with large forward-facing eyes (like humans).

OBSERVATIONS

Owls have excellent hearing and vision. Their eyes are tube-shaped and act as literal binoculars to find their prey. Their eyes can't move, so to see around them they must move their neck, which luckily can rotate 270 degrees.

The feathers on an owl's flat face form what is called a facial disc. These feathers radiate out from around the eyes to the ear canal. This unique pattern captures sound waves and directs them right into the ear canals. This helps an owl know exactly where sounds are coming from.

Owls catch their prey with their strong, sharp talons and eat them whole. They can't digest bones, fur, feathers, and scales so they regurgitate this in a "fur ball" like package called an owl pellet. Finding these pellets can tell you an owl lives nearby and give you a glimpse into what they are eating.

TIP:
Owls will hoot at night to protect territory, so hearing a hoot at night means an owl lives nearby. Bonus tip: Owl feathers are illegal to keep, even if you find them on the ground, so leave them where you find them.

Let's draw a...
SEAGULL

1

2

3

4

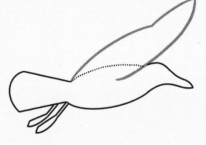

5

6

Seagulls, or just gulls as they are often called, are medium-sized white birds with gray wings. Despite their name, seagulls don't just live by the water, and can be found pretty much anywhere they can find food. Seagulls have very long wings that are edged or tipped in white or black and medium-length black or white tails.

OBSERVATIONS

Seagull beaks are thick, yellow, and hooked at the end, and usually have a red spot on them. They are specially built for picking apart their food. Seagulls are scavengers and will eat mostly anything they can get ahold of, so their beaks come in handy for tearing and picking at their food.

Seagulls have many adaptations to living by the ocean. They are one of few birds that can drink salt water. Special glands near their eyes flush the salt from water and their food and push it out of their bills through their nostrils.

Extra-long wings help make seagulls great fliers. They can still fly expertly in windy conditions and can maneuver in all weather and glide or drift around while looking for food. They have incredible eyesight as well and are one of the few birds whose eyes can move in their sockets, so they can easily spot food while gliding around.

TIP:
Seagulls love to steal your food, so if you are having lunch near a flock, do not leave your food unattended.

Let's draw a...
GREAT BLUE HERON

1

2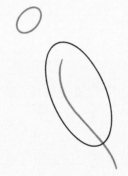

3

4

5

6

Great blue herons are the largest herons in North America. They are grayish-blue with a black stripe of feathers from their eyes to the back of their heads. They have shaggy-looking feather plumes on their head, chest, and wings. They have long legs and sharp long bills. Herons' necks are long and are often held in an "S" shape.

OBSERVATIONS

Great blue heron legs can be almost 2-feet long. Their long legs make it easier for them to wade in the water and not get wet. They have long toes as well, to balance better in wet mud and sand. They can often be seen standing on one leg to keep their other tucked leg warm.

A great blue heron's beak is shaped like a dagger, and they use it like one too. They sit perfectly still and then once they spot their prey, they spear it and swallow it whole. They also use their beaks to stir the water to attract fish to their location.

The fluffy plume of feathers on a great blue heron's chest actually serves a purpose! These feathers fray and turn into a cleaning "down" powder at the ends that a heron combs through with its feet and spreads on its body. The powder cleans off slime and oils from the water and fish.

TIP:
Great blue herons can be found in wetlands all over North America but often stand still like a statue, so look carefully to spot them among the reeds and tall grasses.

Let's draw an...

ARMADILLO

1

2

3

4

5

Armadillos are oval, or bean-shaped animals, with long tapered tails and small pointed heads with large ears on top. They can be found in the Southern United States and South America. They have small black eyes on the side of their heads. Armadillos' bodies are covered in an armored shell that is banded with breaks for better movement.

⊙BSERVATIONS

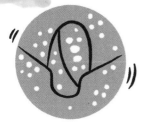

Armadillos, whose name means "little armored one," are covered in a scaly armor called osteoderm. This armor protects them from predators. There are even a few kinds of armadillos that can roll into a ball to protect their body.

Armadillos have long, thick front claws that are perfect for digging. They use them to dig burrows and dig for insects. They can even dig a hole quickly when a predator is near to hide their lower body in and just leave their armor on the top.

Armadillos have long sticky tongues that pull insects out of the ground. They can stick their tongues into an ant nest and slurp up thousands of ants in one meal. They are almost completely blind and deaf, so their good sense of smell helps them find food.

When surprised or scared an armadillo can leap 4 or 5 feet into the air. This behavior usually scares away predators, but also can be dangerous if they jump in front of or underneath a car.

TIP:
Armadillos can be seen in all southern habitats, from desert to water (they are actually great swimmers).

Let's draw an...

AMERICAN BULLFROG

1

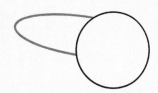

2

3

4

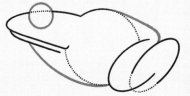

5

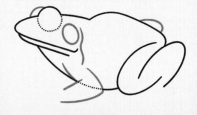

6

The American bullfrog is the largest frog in North America. They can be found in ponds, lakes, and swamps all over the US and Canada. They have varying shades of brown and green on their back and yellow-to-white bellies. Bullfrogs have wide heads with circular eardrums on the sides and long mouths that extend from one side of their head to the other.

OBSERVATIONS

A bullfrog's coloring helps them to camouflage with the plants in their environment. They often have molting, or spots and stripe patterns, for even better camouflage. This keeps them safe from predators and hides them while they are hunting for insects and fish.

The skin on their back is bumpy. These bumps are actually glands that produce a mucus that keeps them from drying out and protects them. These bumps also secrete a poison that tastes bad and deters other animals from eating them.

Bullfrogs' hind legs are long and powerful and have webbed feet. This helps them to swim and jump five times their body length or more (they have been documented jumping over 7 feet).

7 FT+

Bullfrogs have large eyes on the tops of their heads. This allows them to see 180 degrees around them and keep watch. They also have night vision and are one of the only animals that can see colors in complete darkness.

TIP:
When looking for bullfrogs, move slowly so they don't dive underwater. The tops of their heads are often the only thing poking out of the water, so look for their eyes sticking out.

Let's draw a...
RED-EARED SLIDER

1

2

3

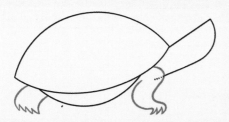

4

5

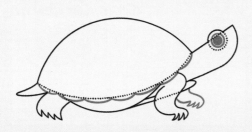

6

CRITTER PROFILE

Red-eared sliders are small-to-medium turtles found in parts of the South and Midwest United States. Their skin color is olive to brown, the top of their shells have yellow stripes, and the bottom of their shells is yellow with dark blotches. The red spot on either side of their head makes them easy to identify. Male red-eared sliders have very long front claws.

OBSERVATIONS

Red-eared sliders are semi-aquatic turtles, which means they spend most of their time in the water. Their webbed feet make them especially good swimmers and they are known to swim in deep water. They can stay underwater for 30–45 minutes before having to take a breath.

A red-eared slider's patterned and striped body is great for camouflaging. This is why they prefer to be in the water, where they blend in and can swim away quickly if they need to escape. They are also able to pull their extremities into their shell, when they feel threatened, to protect them like a shield.

The "slider" part of their name comes from their tendency to slide off rocks and logs quickly into the water. The plastron (or bottom part) of their shell is smooth and flat, making sliding off things fast and effective.

All turtles are attached to their shells, so they do not come off. Turtle shells are made up of scutes. Scutes are bony plates that are fused together. The scutes peel off about once a month as turtles grow, exposing a bigger scute behind.

TIP:
The easiest time to spot red-eared sliders is on sunny days when they sunbathe in groups on logs and rocks poking out of the water (this actually helps kill parasites on their bodies).

Let's draw a...
GARTER SNAKE

1

2

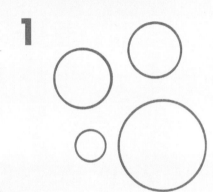

3

4

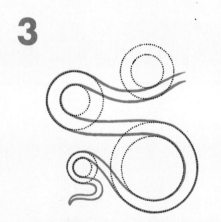

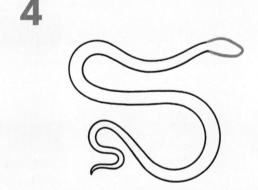

5

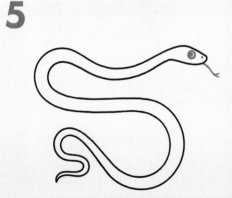

Garter snakes are small harmless snakes found all over North and Central America. They are dark-colored snakes (black, brown, olive) and have three yellow stripes that run the length of their bodies, one down the center of their back with one on either side. Their heads are sleek and the same width as their body, with large round eyes on the sides of their head.

OBSERVATIONS

Garter snakes have long red tongues with a black fork at the end. Their tongues are used for "smelling" the world around them by flicking the air and detecting chemical information that is processed by the nerve endings in the roof of their mouth.

Garter snakes are one of the only snakes that don't lay eggs. Female garter snakes give birth to 20 to 40 babies in one pregnancy but do not take care of them after that. The baby snakes usually go off on their own to hunt within the first hours.

Garter snakes live alone until it is time to hibernate. During hibernation they live in dens with a community of hundreds of other garter snakes to stay warm through the winter.

Garter snakes, bodies are covered in tiny scales that armor their body to protect them from predators and their environment. These scales are made of keratin (the same thing our fingernails are made of) and shed as they grow.

TIP:
Garter snakes are known as a gardener's best friend, because they eat pests that can hurt a garden. They can often be found around gardens on warm afternoons.

Let's draw a...

BLUE-TAILED SKINK

1

2

3

4

5

6

Blue-tailed skinks are small, slender lizards (5- to 8-inches long) found in the Eastern US and Canada. They are often called five-line skinks due to the five white or yellow lines that run from head to tail. The rest of their body is black to dark brown, except for the bright blue tale that young skinks have.

OBSERVATIONS

Young blue-tailed skinks are known for their vibrant blue tails that are sometimes solid blue and sometimes striped. The color of their tail fades as they get older. The blue tail tricks predators into biting it rather than the head of the skink and can detach if they get bit, allowing the skink to get away.

Not only can they detach their tails to escape predators, but blue-tailed skinks can also regrow their tails. The new tail takes about two months to grow back and is usually darker, shorter, and sometimes misshapen.

Blue-tailed skinks are small, so they must rely on adaptation like their detachable tails to stay safe from predators. They are also covered in thick scales to protect themselves, and have sharp claws and a row of tiny sharp teeth. Their claws also come in handy for digging burrows and tunnels to live in, as well as for catching and eating their food such as spiders, insects, snails, and fruits and vegetables.

TIP:
Blue-tailed skinks are cold-blooded and depend on the sun to stay warm. They can be spotted during the day basking in the sun on rocks.

Let's draw a...
RAINBOW TROUT

1

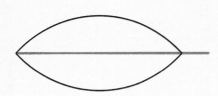

2

3

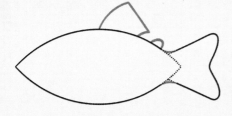

4

5

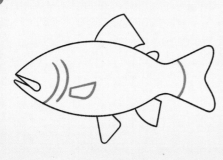

6

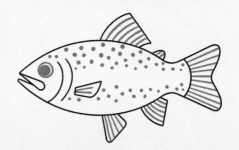

CRITTER PROFILE

Rainbow trout are freshwater fish native to the rivers and lakes in the Western United States (but can now be found throughout the US). Their name comes from their multicolored bodies that can be brown, green, yellow, and iridescent blue, usually with a silvery-white underside and pinkish red stripe on either side. Their body, dorsal fin, and tail are also covered in black, freckle-like spots.

OBSERVATIONS

Rainbow trout are torpedo shaped with a short, rounded snout and long body with a squared tail. They have seven fins: two pectoral fins, two pelvic fins, one anal fin, one dorsal fin, and one adipose fin. They are known to be very fast swimmers and high jumpers. This is due to having a very flexible and muscular body.

Female rainbow trout build nests for their eggs called redds. She will use her tail to fan the gravel away from a shallow area until an area is cleared. This is where she lays her eggs and then lightly covers them in gravel once they have been fertilized.

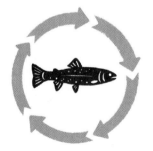

When a rainbow trout is ready to lay eggs, she will come back to the place where she was born. This requires swimming upstream to find her birthplace and build a redd. For some rainbow trout this journey isn't far, but for another kind of rainbow trout called steelheads, this could mean coming from the ocean, which is a long, dangerous journey.

TIP:
Rainbow trout are sensitive to pollution and can only live in clean water, so if you see rainbow trout, it is a good indicator that the water is not polluted.

Let's draw a...
SNAIL

1

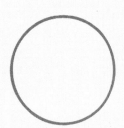

2

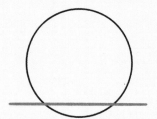

3

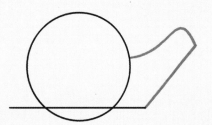

4

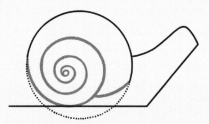

5

6

CRITTER PROFILE

Snails are small yellow-to-brown mollusks with spiral-shaped shells on their backs. Their bodies are long and soft and are mostly inside of their shell except for their head, foot, and tail (which can retract in for protection). They have four tentacles, two long, thin upper tentacles, and two shorter lower tentacles by their mouth.

OBSERVATIONS

The bottom of a snail is called the foot. This is one long muscle located on the belly of the snail. The foot secretes a slimy mucous that helps the snail slide and move around. Snails are very slow, and their movement is called "creeping."

The upper tentacles on a snail head are called eyestalks and are long and thin with an eyeball on the end. Snails can move these stalks around in any direction to see around them without having to move their bodies.

The lower tentacles on a snail head are for smelling and tasting. Snails use these to find food and avoid areas that may be dangerous to them. Below these tentacles is a small mouth filled with thousands of tiny teeth called radula.

Snails build their shells by secreting a material called calcium carbonate out of their mantle (a special organ). Shells all swirl to the right. Their shells are a part of their body that is attached to them, and they never leave it.

TIP:
Snails are nocturnal and love damp dark places like flowerpots, your garden, or under leaves or rocks.

Let's draw a...
DUNGENESS CRAB

1

2

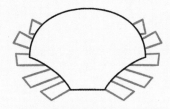

3

4

5

Dungeness crabs are crabs found in the Pacific Ocean along the West Coast of the US. They have broad, hard oval shells that cover their body. They are purplish-gray with cream undersides and legs. Dungeness crabs have four pairs of legs and one pair of large claws. Their eyes are located at the front edge of the shell, as is a mouth.

OBSERVATIONS

Dungeness crabs' mouths have many parts. Many of these mouthparts look like extra legs or little tools, and they help the crab eat the fish and other sea animals it snacks on more easily. Some parts hold the food, some tear it up, and some push the food into the mouth.

Dungeness crabs have long, sharp, spear-like claws. Their claws are extremely powerful, and their pinch is one of the strongest recorded. Their claws are used to catch and break the shells of their food, and the edges are serrated like a saw to tear things open.

Dungeness crabs walk sideways. This is because their legs are located at the sides of their bodies and their joints are sideways, making it easier and quicker for them to just walk side to side. If they want to go forward, they can slowly shuffle but usually prefer not to.

TIP:
The best time to look for Dungeness crabs is low tide, when if you are lucky, you might find one hanging out in the sand or in a tide pool.

Let's draw a...

DAFFODIL

1

2

3

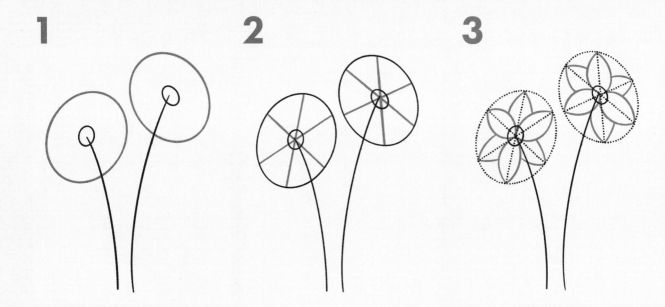

4

5

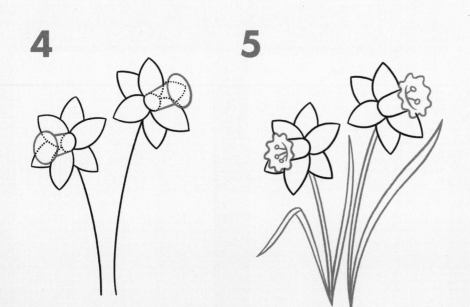

Daffodils are one of the first flowers to bloom in the springtime. They are yellow or white with tall (12-inch) green stems. They have five or six yellow or white leaves with a bright yellow trumpet-like center that ruffles on the ends. They can be seen growing alone, in bunches, or filling a whole field.

OBSERVATIONS

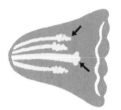

The trumpet-like part of daffodil is sometimes described as a bell and is called a crown or corona. Inside it are the stamen and pistil – the parts necessary for pollination. Pollinators like bees and butterflies fly into corona to drink nectar and pass pollen between flowers.

Daffodils are perennial flowers, which means they come back every year without having to be replanted. They grow from bulbs that look like onions in the ground. They start to bloom in March or April and are one of the first to do so, signaling the start of spring. A field of daffodils can continue to bloom each year for 30 to 50 years!

Daffodils are very poisonous and can kill other plants around them as well as make anything that tries to eat them very sick. This keeps the flower safe from being the food of animals like squirrels and rabbits. All parts of the plant from flower to bulb are poisonous.

TIP:
Daffodils are easy to grow and only need good soil to thrive. Plant daffodil bulbs in the fall to enjoy their beautiful color in the spring.

Let's draw a...
MAPLE LEAF

1

2

3

4

5

OBSERVATIONS

Leaves are used for photosynthesis. Photosynthesis is how a plant uses sunlight, carbon dioxide in the air, and water to make oxygen. Trees' leaves change color and begin to fall off when there is less sunlight during the day to use for photosynthesis, so they go dormant for the winter (kind of like hibernation).

A typical tree leaf is made of a stem, or leaf stalk, that is connected to veins all inside of the blade protected by an epidermis. These veins work just like the veins in our body, transporting nutrients, water, energy, and information throughout the tree.

Leaves are the easiest way to identify a plant. Each kind of plant has unique leaves. Plant leaves are made to capture sunlight and may have a particular shape to best fit the environment it is found in.

Leaves also protect a plant from the elements. They keep the harsh weather from damaging the main trunk or stems of a plant. The leaves of many trees and plants curl up, or even flip over before a storm.

TIP:
Take a nature walk in a local park with your family or explore your backyard to see how many kinds of leaves you can find.

Let's draw a...

CONIFER CONE

1

2

3

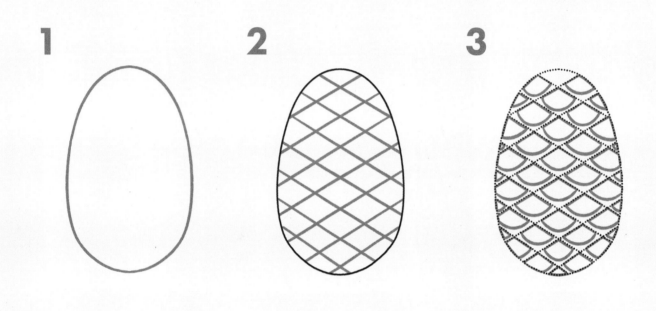

4

5

OBSERVATIONS

Male conifer cones are smaller than the female cones. They are soft and shaped like a small thin oval. Male cones are full of pollen and only exist in the springtime. Wind blows the pollen off the male cones to pollinate female cones, and then the cone dies away.

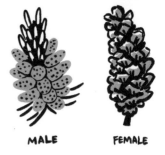

MALE   FEMALE

Female conifer cones are what most people typically think of as pine cones. They are protective wooden cones that have seeds tucked at the base of hard scales. These cones have large scales at the top and smaller scales forming layer on layer until they make a rounded spiky oval. Just like with leaves on deciduous trees, coniferous trees can be identified by their unique cones. A cone's size, shape, color, and texture depend on the type of tree.

During cold, harsh weather, conifer cones close their scales to protect the seeds. When the weather gets warmer, the cone opens, revealing the seeds and allowing them to be pollinated and then release the seeds.

Conifer cones also protect seeds from birds and animals like squirrels that might want to eat them. Many cones have sharp barbs or thorns on them and their woody exterior makes it hard for animals to get through.

TIP:
Look at the base of coniferous trees to find cones. They drop their cones in the fall and can be found scattered around on the ground.

Let's draw a...

POPPY

1

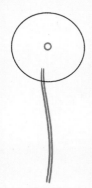

2

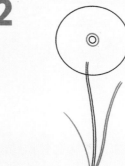

3

4

5

6

A poppy is a bright-colored flower that grows on a tall furry stock. They have four-to-five crepe paper-like petals that form the shape of a cup, with two on top and two or three underneath. Poppies can be many different colors (red, orange, blue, purple, yellow, white), but are most popular in bright red. They have many black or yellow stamens with a thick yellow pistil seedpod in the middle.

OBSERVATIONS

Poppies are full of pollen but do not have any nectar. This still makes them very attractive to pollinators like bees, who eat pollen. Poppy pollen is also very healthy for the bees since it is known to be "clean," which means it doesn't have fungus or toxins.

Poppies have a very short bloom time, with some varieties only lasting a few days and others only up to two weeks. In the southwest US and California, the wild California poppy is known to "super-bloom" after wet winters. Thousands of people travel to see this bloom before it is over.

Poppy seeds come from the poppy flower. After the flower blooms, the petals fall away revealing the seed pod in the middle. This pod can be full of more than 200 seeds. If not harvested, the seeds fall out in slits that open in the pod to spread more flowers the next season.

TIP:
There are over 70 different kinds of poppies, so look at which kind of poppies grow best in your area to plant.

Let's draw a...
DEER MUSHROOM

1

2

3

4

5

6

OBSERVATIONS

The cap of the mushroom protects the gills, which is where the spores of the mushroom are located. Spores are just like seeds and spread to grow more mushrooms.

Deer mushrooms are a fungus. This means they don't get nutrients from the sun like plants and thrive in the dark. Deer mushrooms pull their nutrients from rotting wood that they grow in. They sometimes show up in yards and fields when the soil is made of decomposed wood that is buried. You will often see mushrooms show up after it rains because mushrooms need wet, dark conditions to grow.

Underground, the mushroom has a thread system (like roots) called mycelium. These threads spread all over in the ground and search for nutrients, absorbing it to feed the mushroom. They also communicate with other fungus to connect them all and share nutrients and information.

TIP:
Never pick or eat mushrooms you find unless an adult who knows what they are doing tells you to. Many mushrooms are very poisonous and can even be dangerous to touch.

Let's draw a...
SAGUARO CACTUS

1

2

3

4

5

6

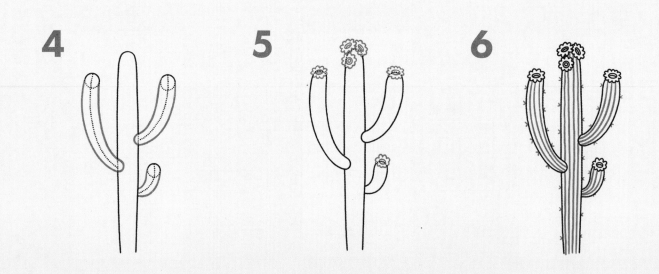

◯BSERVATIONS

Saguaro cactus only grow in the Sonoran Desert located in Arizona, a small part of Southern California, and Mexico. To survive in the desert, these cacti have very thick, waxy skin so they don't lose water through transpiration (similar to sweating).

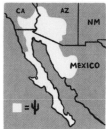

The big spines of the saguaro cactus protect it from animals in the desert. The spines grow all over in starburst clusters with one sharp spine pointing outward in each cluster. They can grow 3 inches long and are very sharp.

Saguaro cacti grow white flowers in the springtime. By summer the flowers turn into a red fruit. People in the Sonoran Desert eat this nutty-tasting food and make sweet foods like jams and candies out of it. The seeds are ground into a flour.

Saguaro cacti are very important for the desert ecosystem and provide a home for many birds, owls, and bats. Rabbits, deer, sheep, and rats all eat the cacti and get water from its flesh.

TIP:
A visit to the Saguaro National Park outside of Tucson, Arizona, is a great place to see saguaro cacti.

Let's draw a...

MONARCH BUTTERFLY

1

2

3

4

5

6

OBSERVATIONS

Monarch butterflies have four scale-covered wings: a pair of forewings and a pair of hindwings. Their wings do not flap but move in a figure-eight pattern when flying. Monarch wings move much slower than most other butterfly wings, flapping only 5 to 12 times a second (instead of 20 times).

Monarch butterflies are known as the milkweed butterfly because the milkweed plant is essential to their survival. They lay their eggs on milkweed plants, their caterpillars only eat milkweed, and when they go through metamorphosis and turn into a butterfly, they drink the milkweed nectar. Milkweed even protects them by making monarch butterflies toxic to animals that try to eat them.

Monarch butterflies migrate incredibly long distances. Each fall, close to a billion monarchs fly thousands of miles south from Canada and the northern United States to spend the winter in Mexico and the southern US. In the spring, they fly back north, laying their eggs on milkweed plants as they go.

TIP:

Picking up a butterfly can damage its wings. You can safely hold a butterfly by dipping a cotton swab in sugar water and allowing the butterfly to land or climb onto it.

Let's draw an...
ANT

1

2

3

4

5

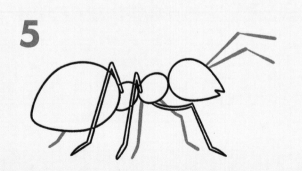

6

Ants are the most common creature on the planet with an estimated 20 quadrillion ants on the Earth. Their bodies are split into three parts: the head, thorax with six legs attached, and the large oval abdomen. Ants have wide heads with mandibles on the end and two long elbowed antennae. They be black, brown, red, and yellow.

OBSERVATIONS

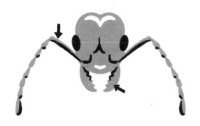

An ant's mandible is one of its best tools. These knife-like pincers in front of their mouth are used for picking up, catching, cutting, and crushing their food. They even use them to fight.

Ants' antennae are long feelers bent at an elbow in front of their head. They use these to touch, taste, and smell. They also use their antennae to communicate with other ants.

Ants are extremely strong and can lift 20 times their body weight (sometimes more depending on the species). They have a lot of muscle in their body compared to their tiny size. Their body is also covered in an exoskeleton, which is a hard armor that keeps them protected.

Ants live in big colonies and each member of the colony has a job. There is a queen, female workers, and the males. Worker ants do many jobs, from building the nest, taking care of the babies, gathering food, and even working as soldiers to protect the colony. Queens lay eggs and male ants are just for mating. In some ant species, the queen and males have wings.

TIP:
If you see an ant, or line of ants, watch where they go to discover their nest.

Let's draw a...
JUMPING SPIDER

1

2

3

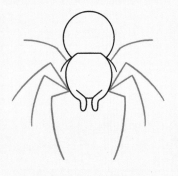

4

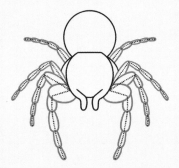

5

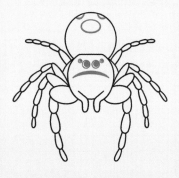

6

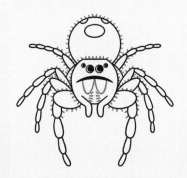

84

CRITTER PROFILE

Jumping spiders are harmless, small furry spiders found all over the world. They have compact bodies, and eight short legs. They can be black, brown, gray, or tan, and often have bright green, yellow, blue, white or red markings. They have iridescent fangs at the front of their mouth and eight eyes with two larger prominent eyes in the center. Jumping-spider markings and colors depend on the species of spider.

OBSERVATIONS

Jumping spiders have pedipalps in the front of their bodies that often make them look like they are waving. These look like extra legs and are used for attracting mates and catching prey. Male pedipalps have rounded ends like boxing gloves.

Like their name suggests, jumping spiders can jump very far (50 times their body length). When they jump, they change the blood flow in their legs until pressure builds and propels them in the direction they want to go. As they jump, they send out a dragline of silk to protect them like a safety net.

Jumping spiders have good hearing and eyesight. They hear using vibrations of sound waves on their hairs. Their large front eyes see in color and great detail, and the other, smaller eyes around their head give them a view of motion around them without having to move their heads.

TIP:
You can carefully trap and observe jumping spiders closely in a terrarium or just a clear cup with breathing holes cut in it. Just remember to let it go when you are done.

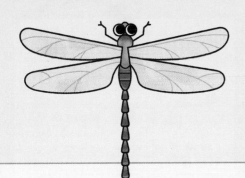

Let's draw a...

DRAGONFLY

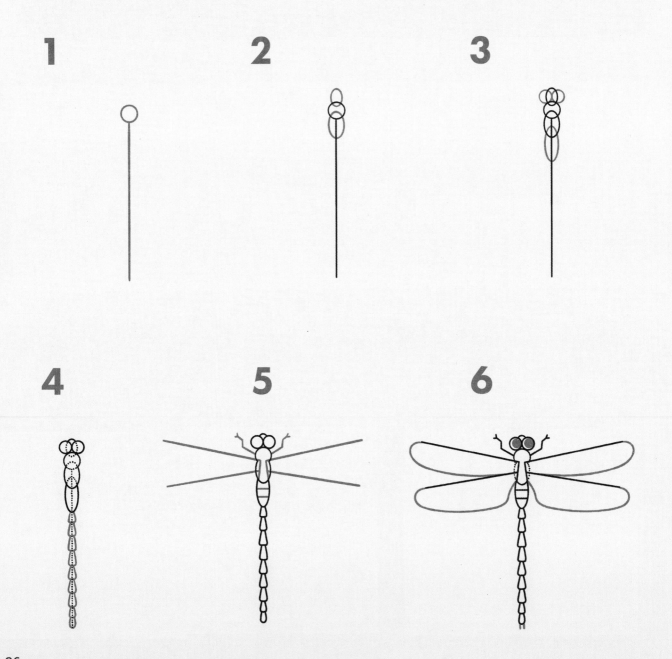

1

2

3

4

5

6

OBSERVATIONS

Dragonflies have massive eyes for great vision. Because most of their head is eyes, they can see almost all the way around them. Dragonflies have much smaller antennae than other insects. They use their antennae to measure air speed while they are flying.

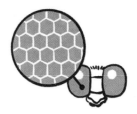

Baby dragonflies, called larvae, are wingless and don't have a long abdomen. They live under the water and eat mosquitoes, other insects, fish, and tadpoles. After a few years in this stage, they climb out of the waters and their exoskeleton opens revealing their abdomen and wings.

Dragonflies rest with their wings out to the sides. Their wings are very flexible and can move separately from each other, making them great fliers. They can fly up, down, and even hover in place.

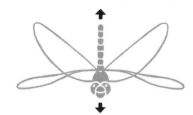

Dragonflies eat their food in the air. They mostly eat other insects and are important for keeping mosquito populations down. One dragonfly can eat hundreds of mosquitoes in one day.

TIP:
Dragonflies are found near any kind of freshwater, and can be spotted on warm sunny days flying or perching on plants near the water.

Let's draw a...

BUMBLEBEE

1

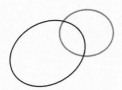

2

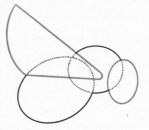

3

4

5

6

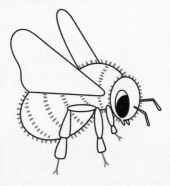

CRITTER PROFILE

A bumblebee is a large fuzzy pollinating insect. They have round bodies and can be almost an inch in length. Their bodies are covered in black-and-yellow striped hair. They have six black legs, a pair of wings, and a small head with two large eyes, three small eyes, and a pair of antennae at the front.

OBSERVATIONS

Not all bumblebees have stingers. The queen and workers have stingers but not the drones. Bumblebees are not aggressive and don't commonly sting unless threatened or protecting their hive.

Bumblebees do not make extra honey like other bees. They collect pollen and nectar and make it into honey for food, but do not store it in a hive. Bumblebees instead live in nests made in abandoned burrows that the queen fills with wax pots for food and eggs.

The buzz sound we hear from a bumblebee is actually the sound of the air vibrating from their wings flapping (230 beats per second). This vibration helps shake pollen off flowers to stick to their hair. It also is a way to warm up or cool down the bumblebee.

Bumblebees communicate with their colony through pheromones (special chemicals). When they find food, they run through their nest, flapping their wings to get the other bumblebees excited.

TIP:
Bumblebees are very important for pollinating our flowers and crops. Planting native plants near your home is the best way to keep them fed and thriving.

Let's draw a...

GRASSHOPPER

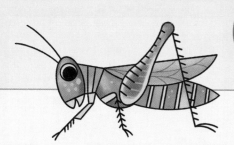

1

2

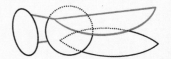

3

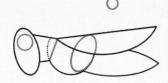

4

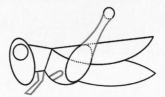

5

6

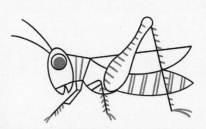

Grasshoppers are large green or brown jumping insects found everywhere in the world except Antarctica. They have a thick oval elongated abdomen, short thorax, and large squared head with a mouthpiece at the end. Grasshoppers have six pairs of feet, two pairs in front and one large pair of hind legs that elbow above their body. Most also have a pair of transparent wings.

OBSERVATIONS

Grasshoppers are herbivores that chew their food. They have special mouthparts called the labrum, mandible, maxilla, and labium that are used like scissors and molars for biting and chewing up plants.

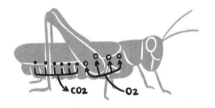

Grasshoppers have five eyes, two big compound eyes, and three small simple eyes. They can see in all directions at once. Their antennae are used for touch and smell. Grasshoppers breathe through holes in their body and hear through eardrums on their bellies.

Grasshoppers use their front pairs of legs for walking, and their large back legs for jumping. They can jump 200 times their body length (sometimes over 20 feet).

Grasshoppers play music with their legs by stridulating. Stridulating is when they rub the pegs on their hind legs against the edges of their wings to make sounds. They do this to attract mates, and to tell other insects that they are in the grasshopper's territory.

TIP:
Grasshoppers often live in meadows or fields. You can find them by walking slowly through the grasses, watching for grasshoppers jumping away as you do.

Let's draw a...

LADYBUG

1

2

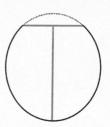

3

4

5

6

CRITTER PROFILE

Ladybugs are small beetles with dome-shaped bodies. Their body is made up of a red or orange split shell that covers its thorax abdomen and wings. Their shell has black spots and sometimes stripes or no markings. They have six short black legs and a black head with a white blotches on either side and a pair of antennas.

OBSERVATIONS

Ladybugs' shells are actually hardened wings. Folded under them for protection is a pair of flying wings that are much larger than their body. When they fly, the shell lifts, exposing the wings that unfold in 0.1 seconds.

Ladybugs are harmless and can be found in trees, shrubs, and gardens. They love to eat aphids, and often lay their eggs under leaves where aphids can be found. Ladybugs are good for gardens because they eat a lot (5,000 insects in their life) and their diet consists of aphids and other pests.

Ladybugs are brightly colored to warn predators that they are not a good meal. When attacked, they secrete a bad-tasting, oily liquid from their legs that makes animals spit them out. If a predator eats them, this liquid is toxic and can make them sick.

Ladybugs hibernate in colonies called a "loveliness of ladybugs" in the winter. Their colonies can have thousands of ladybugs and when one finds a safe place to cluster, they let out a pheromone (chemical) that attracts other ladybugs to the spot.

> ### TIP:
> Look for ladybugs on plant leaves in gardens or fields. Their bright color makes them easy to spot.

Let's draw a...
PRAYING MANTIS

1

2

3

4

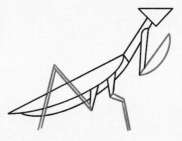

5

6

CRITTER PROFILE

Praying mantises are large insects with recognizable bent front legs. They have long bodies with long necks. Their heads are triangle-shaped with large eyes on either side. Their bodies and wings look like long, thin leaves.

OBSERVATIONS

Praying mantises have six legs: one pair facing forward, one pair facing backward, and one pair held out front. Mantises have extremely fast reflexes and spring their spike-covered front legs out to catch, trap, and pin down their prey.

Praying mantises can turn their head 180 degrees, giving them 360-degree vision, and are the only insect known to see in 3-D. They see best a few inches from their eyes and can process the things they see very quickly, making their reflexes even faster.

Mantises come in many colors to camouflage with the world around them. Their bodies and wings are often shaped like the leaves in their habitat. They can even molt (shed their old skin) to change colors from green to black if necessary.

Only some mantises can fly. These flying mantises are also the only kinds with an ear. This ear, located on their belly, is for detecting the echolocation sounds of bats. The mantis can detect where it is and quickly escape.

TIP:

Praying mantises live in tropical places but can be found in the southern US. They can be spotted on plants where a lot of other bugs live.

FINAL WORDS OF
ENCOURAGEMENT

Isn't nature amazing? Now that you are a seasoned naturalist, you can continue to draw the world around you. Never stop exploring and asking questions!

And remember, if your drawings look different than the ones in this book, that's okay! Your drawings don't have to be perfect. The more you draw, the better you will get. Not to mention it might look different because YOU drew it! There may be a million other people who have drawn this, but no one did it like you!

NATURE JOURNAL

Date: _____ / _____ / _____

Location: _____

Draw what you see:

Describe what you found:

_____
_____
_____
_____
_____

What questions do you have?

_____

_____

_____

_____

_____

Write down three observations:
(What do you smell, hear, feel, see, etc.)

1. _____

2. _____

3. _____

⊙TAKE A CLOSER LOOK

What details do you see when you look closer?

Grab a grown-up and go explore the area around you.

What did you find? Record your observations and draw what you see!

NATURE JOURNAL

Date: _____ / _____ / _____

Location: _____

Draw what you see:

Describe what you found:

_____

_____

_____

_____

What questions do you have?

_____

_____

_____

_____

_____

Write down three observations:
(What do you smell, hear, feel, see, etc.)

1. _____

2. _____

3. _____

⌕ TAKE A CLOSER LOOK

What details do you see when you look closer?

Grab a grown-up and go explore the area around you.

What did you find? Record your observations and draw what you see!

NATURE JOURNAL

Date: /   /

Location:

Draw what you see:

Describe what you found:

What questions do you have?

_____

_____

_____

_____

_____

Write down three observations:
(What do you smell, hear, feel, see, etc.)

1. _____

2. _____

3. _____

TAKE A CLOSER LOOK

What details do you see when you look closer?

Grab a grown-up and go explore the area around you.
What did you find? Record your observations and draw what you see!

NATURE JOURNAL

Date: _____ / _____ / _____

Location: _____

Draw what you see:

Describe what you found:

_____

_____

_____

_____

_____

What questions do you have?

_____

_____

_____

_____

_____

Write down three observations:
(What do you smell, hear, feel, see, etc.)

1. _____

2. _____

3. _____

TAKE A CLOSER LOOK

What details do you see when you look closer?

Grab a grown-up and go explore the area around you.

What did you find? Record your observations and draw what you see!

NATURE JOURNAL

Date: ___/___/___

Location: _____

Draw what you see:

Describe what you found:

_____
_____
_____
_____
_____

What questions do you have?

_____

_____

_____

_____

_____

Write down three observations:
(What do you smell, hear, feel, see, etc.)

1. _____

2. _____

3. _____

⌕AKE A CLOSER LOOK

What details do you see when you look closer?

Grab a grown-up and go explore the area around you.

What did you find? Record your observations and draw what you see!

NATURE JOURNAL

Date: /   /

Location:

Draw what you see:

Describe what you found:

What questions do you have?

_____

_____

_____

_____

_____

Write down three observations:
(What do you smell, hear, feel, see, etc.)

1. _____

2. _____

3. _____

TAKE A CLOSER LOOK

What details do you see when you look closer?

Grab a grown-up and go explore the area around you.

What did you find? Record your observations and draw what you see!

NATURE JOURNAL

Date: _____ / _____ / _____

Location: _____

Draw what you see:

Describe what you found:

_____

_____

_____

_____

_____

What questions do you have?

_____

_____

_____

_____

Write down three observations:
(What do you smell, hear, feel, see, etc.)

1. _____

2. _____

3. _____

TAKE A CLOSER LOOK

What details do you see when you look closer?

Grab a grown-up and go explore the area around you.

What did you find? Record your observations and draw what you see!

NATURE JOURNAL

Date: _____ / _____ / _____

Location: _____

Draw what you see:

Describe what you found:

_____

_____

_____

_____

What questions do you have?

_____

_____

_____

_____

_____

Write down three observations:
(What do you smell, hear, feel, see, etc.)

1. _____

2. _____

3. _____

🔍 TAKE A CLOSER LOOK

What details do you see when you look closer?

Grab a grown-up and go explore the area around you.
What did you find? Record your observations and draw what you see!

NATURE JOURNAL

Date: /   /

Location:

Draw what you see:

Describe what you found:

What questions do you have?

_____

_____

_____

_____

_____

Write down three observations:
(What do you smell, hear, feel, see, etc.)

1. _____

2. _____

3. _____

TAKE A CLOSER LOOK

What details do you see when you look closer?

Grab a grown-up and go explore the area around you.

What did you find? Record your observations and draw what you see!

NATURE JOURNAL

Date: ___ / ___ / ___

Location: _____

Draw what you see:

Describe what you found:

_____
_____
_____
_____
_____

What questions do you have?

_____

_____

_____

_____

_____

Write down three observations:
(What do you smell, hear, feel, see, etc.)

1. _____

2. _____

3. _____

TAKE A CLOSER LOOK

What details do you see when you look closer?

Grab a grown-up and go explore the area around you.
What did you find? Record your observations and draw what you see!

NATURE JOURNAL

Date: _____ / _____ / _____

Location: _____

Draw what you see:

Describe what you found:

_____

_____

_____

_____

_____

What questions do you have?

_____

_____

_____

_____

_____

Write down three observations:

(What do you smell, hear, feel, see, etc.)

1. _____

2. _____

3. _____

⊙AKE A CLOSER LOOK

What details do you see when you look closer?

Grab a grown-up and go explore the area around you.

What did you find? Record your observations and draw what you see!

NATURE JOURNAL

Date: _____ / _____ / _____

Location: _____

Draw what you see:

Describe what you found:

_____

_____

_____

_____

_____

What questions do you have?

_____

_____

_____

_____

Write down three observations:
(What do you smell, hear, feel, see, etc.)

1. _____

2. _____

3. _____

TAKE A CLOSER LOOK

What details do you see when you look closer?

Grab a grown-up and go explore the area around you.

What did you find? Record your observations and draw what you see!

NATURE JOURNAL

Date: _____ / _____ / _____

Location: _____

Draw what you see:

Describe what you found:

_____
_____
_____
_____
_____

What questions do you have?

_____

_____

_____

_____

_____

Write down three observations:
(What do you smell, hear, feel, see, etc.)

1. _____

2. _____

3. _____

TAKE A CLOSER LOOK
What details do you see when you look closer?

Grab a grown-up and go explore the area around you.
What did you find? Record your observations and draw what you see!

NATURE JOURNAL

Date: _____ / _____ / _____

Location: _____

Draw what you see:

Describe what you found:

_____

_____

_____

_____

_____

What questions do you have?

_____

_____

_____

_____

Write down three observations:
(What do you smell, hear, feel, see, etc.)

1. _____

2. _____

3. _____

TAKE A CLOSER LOOK

What details do you see when you look closer?

Grab a grown-up and go explore the area around you.

What did you find? Record your observations and draw what you see!

NATURE JOURNAL

Date: _____ / _____ / _____

Location: _____

Draw what you see:

Describe what you found:

_____

_____

_____

_____

_____

What questions do you have?

_____

_____

_____

_____

Write down three observations:
(What do you smell, hear, feel, see, etc.)

1. _____

2. _____

3. _____

TAKE A CLOSER LOOK

What details do you see when you look closer?

Grab a grown-up and go explore the area around you.

What did you find? Record your observations and draw what you see!

Photography Credits

Crow - Bruce A Clifton/Shutterstock.com

Mallard - Georgi Tsachev/Shutterstock.com

Eagle - PHOTOOBJECT/Shutterstock.com

Praying mantis - Ryzhkov Oleksandr/Shutterstock.com

Ladybug - Mironmax Studio/Shutterstock.com

Grasshopper - Chase D'animulls/Shutterstock.com

Bee - HeatherJane/Shutterstock.com

Dragonfly - Cliff Day/Shutterstock.com

Spider - Rico Andreas/Shutterstock.com

Ant - Dreamland Photography/Shutterstock.com

Butterfly - CHAINFOTO24/Shutterstock.com

Cactus - Traveller70/Shutterstock.com

Mushroom - Vladys Creator/Shutterstock.com

Poppy - UniquePhotoArts/Shutterstock.com

Pinecone - Chris Redan/Shutterstock.com

Maple leaf - ju_see/Shutterstock.com

Daffodil - tonkid/Shutterstock.com

Crab - Jennifer Nicole Buchanan/Shutterstock.com

Snail - Zebra-Studio/Shutterstock.com

Trout - Cannon Colegrove/Shutterstock.com

Skink - IrinaK/Shutterstock.com

Snake - Amrad/Shutterstock.com

Slider - Simon_g/Shutterstock.com

Frog - Joe McDonald/Shutterstock.com

Armadillo - Tim Herbert/Shutterstock.com

Heron - Joseph Scott Photography/Shutterstock.com

Seagull - ForGaby/Shutterstock.com

Owl - Alan Tunnicliffe/Shutterstock.com

Blue Jay - FotoRequest/Shutterstock.com

Robin - Janet M Kessler/Shutterstock.com

Bat - Rudmer Zwerver/Shutterstock.com

Skunk - Layne VR/Shutterstock.com

Moose - Dan Gaura/Shutterstock.com

Bear - Volodymyr Burdiak/Shutterstock.com

Rabbit - Geza Farkas/Shutterstock.com

Racoon - Vladimir Wrangel/Shutterstock.com

Fox - RT Images/Shutterstock.com

Squirrel - My Generations Art/Shutterstock.com

Beaver - Jody Ann/Shutterstock.com

Deer - Holly Kuchera/Shutterstock.com